Contents

Preface

The period between 2008 and 2010 was significant in Southeast Asia. During this period, the Association of Southeast Asian Nations (ASEAN) Charter came into force. The idea of one economic, political, and socio-cultural community for the 10 Member-States was ever more inching closer to reality. While this was unfolding, I was able to witness this community-building process by being at the ASEAN Secretariat in Jakarta, Indonesia in 2008 and at the ASEAN Centre for Biodiversity in 2009-2010.

This collection of essays revisits the significant events, burning issues, and memorable times in ASEAN and so in Indonesia in 2008-2010. They attempt to shed light on these events, issues and rekindle the times when nationalistic and regionalistic fervor was at the peak.

There are five topics that organize the essays. The first one is on regional studies. It starts with the banner year, 2008, for ASEAN when the new Secretary-General, Dr. Surin Pitsuwan, took his office and the role of the regional organization in the humanitarian operations and reconstruction projects in Myanmar in the post-Cyclone Nargis. One essay questions the inclusiveness of the regional integration process of the envisioned one ASEAN community when it comes to peoples participation in the process. The last essay on this topic is the security threat posed by North Korea and how ASEAN can address the threat.

The second topic deals with the environmental issues. Two essays focus on both the regional trends that cause problems and the regional capabilities and structures that can buck the trends.

The third topic is on the political developments in Indonesia. The Commission for Truth and Friendship (CTF) report is examined and its contextual usefulness. Then, the second presidential victory by Susilo Bambang Yudhoyono (SBY) is put into a global political perspective by looking at the wave of victories of oppositions in various national politics.

In the fourth topic, national security issues are discussed. In 2008, the streets of Jakarta saw the violence of

2

student protests. At the other side of the violence are the works of the government. The last essay in the national security issues describes the deadly stampede which is a symptom of social injustice and structural violence in the country.

The last topic is on the nationalistic fervor and travel insights. Celebrating Independence Day and winning an Olympic gold generate emotional attachment to the flag and nation. Being in Jakarta, masjids and gerejas are landmarks which offer not only religious symbol, but spiritual refuge as well. Writing Jakarta without any mention of traffic jams and motorcycles is prejudicial to what it really is.

Most of these essays were published in The Jakarta Post in 2008-2010.

The banner year, 2008, for the ASEAN Way

In Southeast Asia, there is a prevailing community-like approach to decision-making and dealing with issues affecting the region. It is known as the ASEAN Way, which is based on consensus.

Early in 2008, the ASEAN Secretariat had a new Secretary General, Dr. Surin Pitsuwan from Thailand. He came to the organization with a clear vision and direction.

It was his idea to have a festival of performing arts to bring ASEAN peoples together. Thus, the Best of ASEAN Performing Arts had an inaugural presentation entitled "The Mosaic Archipelago" last May 6-7. The second feature for the Best ASEAN Performing Arts was held last August 8 which was the 41st founding anniversary of ASEAN. Diplomats from various countries, Indonesian government officials, and ASEAN citizens were gathered together to be awed by "The Tapestry of Thai Beauty and Grace." Both presentations from Indonesia and Thailand were made open to the ASEAN public for free. There will be more presentations from the eight remaining member-states. This kind of presentations is aimed to raise awareness of ASEAN and its mission in the region and foster appreciation and understanding of the region's rich and diverse performing arts.

Another crowning achievement of the ASEAN was the approval of the ASEAN Charter in the 2007 Singapore Summit. The ASEAN Charter has been ratified by seven member-states. The three remaining member-states which have yet to ratify the Charter are now in the process of ratification in their respective national legislative bodies. It is expected that the Charter will be ratified by all member-states by the end of the year 2008, in time for the Bangkok Summit. The Charter stipulates about building three communities; Economic Community, Political and Security Community and Socio-Cultural Community. The Economic Community has already adopted a blueprint that would guide the strategic and key actions of the community. However, the other two communities are in the process of drafting their blueprints in final forms to be adopted in the 2008 Bangkok Summit. Meetings to improve the draft of blueprints for the two communities were held in September 2008. Drafters are optimistic that the final draft will be ready for adoption in the 2008 Bangkok Summit.

In May 2008, Cyclone Nargis introduced an important role to ASEAN for the early recovery and reconstruction of one of its member-states, Myanmar (Burma). At first, the government of Myanmar allowed little foreign humanitarian aid and relief workers into the country. This unfortunate posturing of Myanmar stirred controversies which got into the way of humanitarian assistance to the victims and survivors of Cyclone Nargis. The ASEAN Secretariat set up a coordinating office which forms part of the Tripartite Core Group (TCG) composed of the Government of the Union of Myanmar, United Nations, and ASEAN. The TCG is based in Yangon, Myanmar and has humanitarian operations in the hardest hit Ayeyarwady Delta and Yangon Divisions. The TCG reported that Cyclone Nargis brought about 84,537 deaths and 53,836 people missing. The magnitude and extent of casualties and damages to properties prompted the international community to hold the ASEAN-UN International Pledging Conference which took place on May 25, 2008. The conference paved the way for the formation of TCG and the conduct of Post-Nargis Joint Assessment (PONJA) which formed the basis for the humanitarian and relief operations in the Delta region. The ASEAN Secretariat leads the coordinating task of TCG while Myanmar chairs it. Through this breakthrough, UN agencies such as United Nations Children's Fund (UNICEF), UN High Commissioner for Refugees (UNHCR), World Health Organization (WHO), World Food program (WFP), and other international relief and humanitarian organizations were able to operate in the affected areas of Delta Region. One UNOCHA officer, Jarle Tverli, based in Bogale Township said, "If not for ASEAN, UN agencies would not have been here in the Delta Region."

The TCG has designed and conducted a Community-Based Early Recovery Project in Seik Gyi Village, Kunyangon Township in Yangon Division which was heavily affected by Cyclone Nargis. The project is groomed as a model village project for early recovery with robust livelihood components such as growing betel leaves and providing boats and nets for

5

fishing. ASEAN volunteers in close coordination with the villagers are the ones implementing this project. The projects of the TCG in which the ASEAN was the lead organization helped in rebuilding and reconstructing the communities heavily affected by the Cyclone Nargis.

With the ratification of the ASEAN Charter, the ASEAN is moving towards a rule-based organization. This is expected to step up the integration and cooperation efforts and expound more the ASEAN Way to effectively deal with regional affairs.

With Dr. Surin Pitsuwan, ASEAN Secretary-General, during the Second ASEAN Best Performing Arts in Jakarta, Indonesia in 2008

ASEAN citizens, key to regional integration process

Coincidentally and significantly, the two most known regional organizations in the world -- the European Union (EU) and the Association of Southeast Asian Nations (ASEAN) -- are currently ratifying their instrumental agreements to bind and integrate their member states more, economically, politically, socially and legally.

The EU has the Lisbon Treaty up for ratification. Its 27 member states must ratify the treaty for it to be in force. Thus far, 19 member states have approved the treaty in their parliaments, except in Ireland where the treaty was subjected to a referendum because of constitutional obligations. Irish voters rejected the treaty, with 53.4 percent of voters saying "no". As a result, the treaty is technically frozen while the other member states, which have not yet approved the treaty, proceed with their ratification processes.

On the other hand, ASEAN, which will celebrate its 41st founding anniversary on Aug. 8, has the binding ASEAN Charter subject to ratification by its 10 member states.

Thus far, Myanmar became the seventh member state to ratify the ASEAN charter joining Brunei, Cambodia, Laos, Malaysia, Singapore and Vietnam.

The Philippines, Indonesia and Thailand have approved the charter, but they have indicated that their ratification heavily depends on the improvement of Myanmar's human rights record. This pronouncement by the three original member states of the 40-year-old regional organization raised doubts on the fate of the charter, which is seen to be vital to the integration and cooperation processes of the region, aspiring to live up to its slogan: "One Vision, One Identity, One Community."

Undeniably, the two regional organizations aim to unite and build a community of diverse peoples into one dynamic system. The processes and effectiveness of unification or union and community building does not come about without the cooperation and sense of ownership of the peoples involved. The Irish vote pointedly stresses this.

Although these regional organizations are intergovernmental organizations, the governments in the regional blocs emanate their power from their own peoples. Without the peoples' consent and will, the acts of the governments can be rendered illegitimate, undemocratic and cannot stand for long in the unforgiving scrutiny of history.

The significance of the role of the peoples in the government cannot be ignored in the integration and cooperation processes in a regional organization. However, it is often understood that these regional organizations are composed of governments run by their own peoples through representative governments. It is assumed that an act of government reflects the will of its peoples or at least the majority of them. Most often than not, the governments have their own mind detached from the peoples' heart.

Both the EU and ASEAN point to a location, position and region on the global map. In human geography, there is a humanist's perspective of a region being a source of identification and meaning. Thus, Southeast Asia and Europe are not simply geographical units, but social constructs as well, where peoples identify themselves and create meanings for themselves.

Now, the commonalities between EU and ASEAN stop there.

The European Union is able to institutionalize formal structures that perform state's functions. Rulemaking infrastructures and institutions have been established to govern the dynamic process of European economic, political and social integration. The peoples of Europe have become EU citizens. Well, that is Europe. That is the EU.

In ASEAN, its Charter states that community building would be established in an ASEAN Community comprising the ASEAN Security Community, the ASEAN Economic Community and the Socio-Cultural Community through improved regional cooperation and integration.

Anthropologically, a community emerges when, among its peoples, there exist meaningful and patterned interactions that provide value and significance to their existence and membership in the community.

Basically, these patterned interactions among the peoples are builders of social institutions. For example, since the founding of ASEAN in 1967, patterned interactions among the leaders of member states have been the discussion of issues and opportunities for collaboration.

The regularity of interaction among member states led to the creation of the ASEAN Secretariat in 1976 to coordinate the implementation and ensure the efficiency of various ASEAN projects and programs. The ASEAN Secretariat has now become an institution.

To broaden a community, enhanced interaction among its target peoples is necessary. This can be done by bringing the target peoples together. And what bring the peoples together, are rituals and cultural presentations of other peoples. As the Secretary-General of ASEAN, Surin Pitsuwan, said, "Through culture, we can bring the peoples of ASEAN closer together."

The contact hypothesis in peace and conflict studies has shown that by bringing peoples together and in contact with each other, tends to lessen the chance of conflict. It also fosters knowledge of other peoples and heightens understanding among the peoples.

Hence, ASEAN peoples must have more opportunities to gather together. One opportunity is coming this August on the anniversary of ASEAN. Thailand will feature its dances and puppetry shows here in Jakarta on ASEAN Day.

With this opportunity, ASEAN is putting the peoples through their culture at the center stage of integration process as a community. After all, it is the peoples that comprise a community and not governments, investments nor development plans.

Trusting North Korea: ASEAN paving the way

North Korea's nuclear test destroyed the core requirement for the resumption of the six-party talks - trust. The underground explosion of a reportedly 15-kiloton nuclear bomb, comparable to the atomic bombs that were dropped on Nagasaki and Hiroshima at the end of World War II, crushed any hopes that diplomacy would bring North Korea back to the talks and eventually disable its nuclear program. Can the global community still trust North Korea?

US President Barack Obama called the nuclear test "blatant defiance" of the UN Security Council's resolution and international law. British Prime Minister Gordon Brown condemned the test and described it as "erroneous, misguided, and a danger to the world." Japanese Prime Minister Taro Aso saw it as a "grave challenge" and the president of South Korean said it was "provocation."

Indeed, it is a global security and peace concern. But the global community can not simply renew isolation of and sanctions against North Korea. Isolation and sanctions, time and again, have not brought the desired outcome. The six-party talks, which include the US, Russia, Japan, South Korea, and China, have likewise been fairly ineffective in persuading North Korea to abandon its nuclear program. UN and world leaders need to come up with a more creative response to this latest antagonism against global security and peace. Military action is not this creative response.

In 2006, North Korea's first nuclear test surprised the global community. Prior to that, it was widely known that the poor country was developing a nuclear bomb. Little did the world know that such an impoverished country could create the dreaded nuclear bomb so quickly and with such a degree of success. North Korea joined the elite nuclear-armed countries, the fourth in Asia to explicitly announce its successful nuclear test.

Despite its impoverishment, North Korea was bent on pursuing its nuclear ambition that momentous year of 2006. It acknowledged that the ambition to be a nuclear-armed country was a way to gain respect in the global community and exalt the pride of North Koreans amidst their daily hardships. It recognized the power and leverage of nuclear bomb in international relations. When things were bad for North Korea, a nuclear test seemed to rouse the nationalism of its own people. It should be noted that North Korea's 67-year old reclusive leader, Kim Jong-Il, reportedly suffered a stroke last year.

Prior to the latest nuclear test, North Korea was lambasted for launching a satellite into orbit. Many believed that it was testing a long-range missile with the aim of reaching US soil. The UN Security Council strongly criticized the launching. North Korea demanded an apology from the world community for what is said was the confusion of a rightful and peaceful space development program with a military exercise.

With no apology from the UN in sight, North Korea unilaterally ditched the six-nation talks and threatened to enable its nuclear program. North Korea was still demanding an apology from the UN at the eleventh hour. Left with one option to redeem its position on the international arena, North Korea daringly conducted its nuclear test. This time the bomb was bigger and more powerful than the one launched in 2006. It effectively caught the attention of the global community.

Reports say that the belligerent country has also tested short-range and medium-range missiles.

In the midst of these developments, a number of diplomats, including US Secretary of State Hillary Clinton, are encouraging North Korea to rejoin the six-nation talks and uphold its 2007 commitment to disable its nuclear program.

In 2007, North Korea agreed to denuclearization in exchange for 1 million tons of fuel and other concessions, including its removal from the US' *axis of evil'. There were disagreements as to how to proceed with the agreement, particularly as to how to verify North Korea's disarmament.

The commitments by all parties in the talks were only partly fulfilled. The 1-million tons of fuel oil was not delivered in full, prompting North Korea to demand its delivery before it would allow US to verify its disarmament. Other political and historical factors contributed to the bungled implementation of the agreement in 2007.

11

So can the global community still trust North Korea? And can North Korea trust the global community?

As the convener of the ASEAN Regional Forum, in which North Korea is a member, ASEAN, being a Zone of Peace, Freedom and Neutrality (ZOPFAN) can facilitate the reopening of talks with North Korea. The ASEAN Secretariat in Indonesia can be instrumental and key to the preventive diplomacy in the Korean peninsula and potentially the Asia-Pacific region.

Fulfillment of the previously made commitments would build trust and encourage the resumption of talks. After all, trust is the heart of any talks or negotiations. Sadly, this trust was shattered by the recent nuclear test. ASEAN can pick up the pieces and act as a forum for open dialogue.

Earth Day in a regional perspective

"All the regions of the Philippines; the Mekong River Delta in Vietnam; almost all the regions of Cambodia; the North and East of the Lao PDR; the Bangkok region of Thailand; and West Sumatra, South Sumatra, West Java and East Java of Indonesia are all among the most vulnerable regions in Southeast Asia." These are the conclusions of a study entitled "Climate Change Vulnerability Mapping for Southeast Asia" by the Economic and Environment Program for Southeast Asia (EEPSEA) in 2009.

There were three factors considered in the study to identify these climate change "hotspots," namely, climatic hazards (floods, droughts, cyclones, etc.), human and ecological sensitivity (population density and protected areas), and adaptive capacities (socio-economic data, technology and infrastructure).

Climate change, as we know, is one of the biggest threats to biodiversity. Conservation International (CI) identified the areas called biodiversity hotspots in dire need of conservation and protection due to high prevalence of species and high risks.

Of the 34 biodiversity hotspots in the world identified by CI, Southeast Asia hosts four of these; Indo-Burma, the Philippines, Sundaland (Borneo and Sumatra), and Wallacea (Sulawesi and Moluccas). These biodiversity hotspots are home to thousands of endemic species, some of which are threatened and endangered.

With climate change ever threatening our rich regional biodiversity, as concerned ASEAN citizens, what can we do in our endeavors to conserve and protect our biodiversity?

Global environmental issues and concerns such as climate change and biodiversity loss are covered by Multilateral Environmental Agreements (MEAs) to address such issues. For example, the issue of climate change is tackled by the United Nations Framework Convention on Climate Change (UNFCC) while biodiversity loss is covered by the Convention on Biological Diversity (CBD).

13

If there is one measure that can be credited for slowing down global environmental degradation and promoting global environmental vigilance and care, then it is, I must say, the collection of MEAs which are legally binding on the countries who signed these environmental conventions.

Although there still exist tremendous challenges to combat global environmental problems, the MEAs have shown the achievements, limitations and potentiality of these agreements to confront pressing and complex global environmental issues such as threats to biodiversity. MEAs have laid a good foundation and framework for policy and actions by decision-makers, if we intend to really do something on biodiversity conservation.

For activists, MEAs have provided a good starting point for discussion, debate, criticism and action. As citizens of signatory Parties, which are our governments, we are called upon to advance the goal of protecting and conserving our Earth from human destructiveness and greed. We should push our governments to help them comply with their obligations to prevent and manage negative human impacts on the Earth.

The current political-economic situation in our region and even in the world may not look conducive to significant reforms to highlight environmental protection and conservation, but the reports of EEPSEA on climate change "hotspots" may trigger responses and key actions from governments, private sector and NGOs.

Various national problems in the region bring us to the challenges facing regional structures. As we know, regional environmental issues and concerns are not insulated from national political and economic problems facing member states. New elections in Indonesia mean a new government and new directions, whilst economic recession is affecting Singapore.

There is an impending election in the Philippines, along with political uncertainties in Thailand and Myanmar. Malaysia also has a new leader and government. These are the changing realities in the region, affecting the efforts and directions we may take in protecting and conserving the Earth from the negative impacts of climate change and other environmental hazards.

There are logical reasons to look beyond countries and nation-states to determine adequate responses to the social, political, economic and environmental realities that challenge us. We must examine and push forward regional structures such as ASEAN to play a more enhanced role in addressing transnational concerns and issues.

Regional structures can represent and articulate collective interests and, at the same time, manage collective affairs and obligations of member states in regional and global levels.

The power and jurisdiction in tackling environmental concerns and issues must not rest solely on individual governments.

Various actors such as NGOs, the private sector and individuals have shown and proven their contributions in combating and mitigating climate change. These partnerships within countries and beyond can open up environmental possibilities from which we can draw valuable lessons.

Regional structures, such as the ASEAN Centre for Biodiversity (ACB), can offer cooperative problem-solving mechanisms bringing together ASEAN member states to provide our Earth with a breathing space in the midst of choking challenges such as climate change and biodiversity loss.

ASEAN is blessed with rich biodiversity. Millions of tourists from all over the world come to our region to witness and enjoy this richness. Let us help our region protect and conserve its biodiversity. Let us have one region on Earth that showcases the beauty and wonders of biodiversity - let it be ASEAN.

Challenges in population, urbanization and environment

Pressing global challenges such as climate change, poverty and food insecurity are essentially human-induced problems. There are approximately 6.77 billion people in the world today, and the global population is still growing at a rate of 1.14 percent annually.

That equates to nearly 80 million new individuals on this planet every year. At the current rate, projections indicate that by 2015 there will be 7.2 billion people inhabiting earth.

Southeast Asia, including East Timor, is home to more than 574 million people. Indonesia is theworld's fourth most populous country, largest Muslim country and the third biggest democracy.

It alone makes up more than a third of the entire population of the region. Four members of the ASEAN are in the top 24 most populous countries, while most have higher birth rates and greater population densities (bar Laos) than the global average.

Today, urban areas comprise of more than half the world's population. Urbanization has been a global phenomenon that transforms not only land use but people's values and lifestyles. The influx of people for rural areas into the city in search of a better life is too astounding to put into figures.

By 2015, according to UN Population Fund (UNFPA), there will be three cities in Southeast Asia with more than 10 million inhabitants, known as mega cities Jakarta (17.3 million), Metro Manila (14.8 million) and Bangkok (10.1 million).

These sprawling urban areas and enormous populations exert a tremendous amount of stress on the environment. Resources are heavily concentrated in urban areas, causing major challenges in waste disposal, noise, air and water pollution, soil erosion, deforestation and many others.

As a result the environment, particularly biodiversity, is under constant threat. Mega cities are a major source of greenhouse gases emissions, which cause global warming.

Human activities and consumption patterns, coupled with industrial and commercial concentrations in these cities, drain resources found in urban and neighbouring areas. They also compromise the environmental conditions of these areas.

The current population trend is definitely bearing an adverse impact on the quality of natural resources, such as water, food, forest and air. There is a global shortage of potable water and food.

The world's forest areas are shrinking. The quality of air in some cities is leading to health problems in certain people. The current condition of the environment is barely sustainable enough to maintain a decent human existence.

Despite all the challenges we face, it is humans who are ultimately responsible for this destruction to our natural environment. Constantly increasing the global population is not a good step toward tackling this issue. It may help win an election, but it will not win the struggle for a better life on earth.

Population trends, urbanization and environmental challenges demand comprehensive and long-term policy responses from concerned governments.

Policies cannot change the past, but they can shape the future by providing direction toward a better scenario. With the support of international and local NGOs and donors, governments recognizing the extent of these pressing global challenges can act on measures disrupting population trends and declining birth rates.

To do this, there is a need to expand the access and choices of women in education, economic opportunities, political participation and social integration. Studies show that women with higher education tend to have fewer children. Women enjoying economic, political and social freedom tend to give birth later in life. Men too need to be given responsibility to better manage this reproductive power.

Another measure that can be taken by governments is the distribution of economic opportunities to rural areas. The myth that a better life can only be found in the city should be squashed. This measure will halt the influx of rural people to urban areas. Moreover, development planning and process should not be heavily concentrated on urban areas.

These measures could relieve the environmental conditions from degeneration. With population and urbanization being checked, global challenges such as climate change, poverty and food insecurity can be tackled effectively. The question is, are our world's leaders up to the challenge? We, as those solely responsible for the problem, should be proactive in encouraging our leaders to respond to these problems. Otherwise, the future generations will blame us forever.

Reporting the Commission for Truth and Friendship (CTF) report

Post-conflict scenarios are sensitive in context and history. Timor Leste is undergoing that scenario. Indonesia is looking through that same scenario.

By the very name of the commission, the Commission for Truth and Friendship (CTF), I would not pin any hopes on apology, forgiveness, justice, reconciliation and social healing taking place with the findings and recommendations of the commission's final report. However, the uncovering of facts related to the violence before, during and after the referendum in East Timor in 1999 sets the groundwork for any attempt and effort to restore, rebuild and reclaim the losses and damages brought about by the violence.

Those facts are truth. They hurt some people. They also liberate others.

Some people are satisfied with the CTF report. At least for them, truth was made public and confirmed the reports of gross human rights violations in that fateful year of 1999 for East Timor and Indonesia. These people wanted to close the book of that chapter of history. They wanted both countries to move on, (toward what?). Others are concerned of where to go and what's next with the knowledge of truth. The sense of restlessness with the knowledge of truth has taken root and cannot be denied to grow and flourish.

I would not explore the painful part of truth; rather, I would open up the liberating aspect of truth which will burst into positive possibilities for both countries and their people.

It is the possession of the knowledge of truth that will start the processes of apology, forgiveness, justice and reconciliation leading to social healing. All of these processes have sociopolitical dimensions. While it is true that these processes arise mostly in the private sphere, which is mainly a subjective experience, there have been instances where these processes were seen in the public arena, which is primarily sociopolitical in nature.

I heard President Susilo Bambang Yudhoyono expressing his deep regret after receiving the final CTF report. I also heard the Pope Benedict XXVI apologizing for the sexual abuses of the clergies in the United States and Australia. I recall the apology of Prime Minister Rudd of Australia for the injustices committed against the aborigines by the Australian government and its people.

These are symbolic and political acts. They are also vicarious ones. President SBY, Pope Benedict XXVI and Prime Minister Rudd are not the ones who committed the wrongdoings. They were acting on behalf of the offenders.

How can forgiveness be given then? Forgiveness is given to real and individual offenders and not to nameless and faceless collectives. Where are they?

This is where the report of the CTF becomes significant in East Timor's post-conflict scenario. The report holds both parties of the conflict responsible for the violence. The leaders and commanders of troops should make the apology on behalf of the troops and militias who committed the atrocities on the ground.

Most often than not, apologies do not come easily because both parties tend to claim to be the victims and not the offenders, and the offenders see nothing wrong in their acts. Those acts, as told, were by the books.

If made, the process of apology demands three things, namely the admission of wrongdoing, being sorry for the wrongdoing and restoring something that was wronged. It is then that forgiveness is possible.

Forgiveness can also be proactive, as in the case of Nelson Mandela. As a victim of brutal apartheid, he famously forgave those behind it and his imprisonment, ahead of the set-up of the Truth Commission of South Africa.

Forgiveness is in the hands of the offended -- victims and survivors of the atrocities. Where are they in this case? Have we listened to their stories?

Along with forgiveness, the destructive feeling and thinking of revenge and bitterness are transformed into trust and acceptance of history, truth and the differences in ideology, ethnicity, religion and class which oftentimes provoke people to commit violence against others.

However, forgiving prematurely may do more harm than good. The readiness and knowledge of what is to forgive are essential to the process of forgiveness.

Another process essential to a post-conflict scenario is sociopolitical justice which is largely about treating an individual or group fairly and lawfully. Any breach in treating an individual or group fairly and lawfully is a form of injustice that has to be rectified and prevented by the process of justice.

There are two types of justice, retributive and restorative. Retributive justice pertains to something that is intended to repay the wrongdoing, while restorative justice refers to something that restores the state of the person or group injured and offended by the wrongdoing.

The CTF cannot dispense justice. That is for a judicial body, an international tribunal or special court created to hear the cases of gross human rights violations. I will not recommend a regular court to try these cases for obvious reasons. The International Criminal Court based in The Hague, Netherlands, is an example of a judicial body that is created and mandated to hear cases of crimes against humanity and the like.

After justice is rendered, the process of reconciliation acts as the overriding and integrative element of processes of forgiveness, apology and justice toward social healing. It normalizes relations between the two parties.

Have there ever been normal relations between Timor Leste and Indonesia?

What I have just presented are the positive possibilities and liberating aspects of truth that we have now in our midst.

Whether they happen or not, I am convinced that truth will settle its weight on a positive note.

Opposition wave in the global politics: Not in Indonesia

When the Group of Eight (G8) met in Canada in 2010, the group had three new faces. Japan, Australia, and United Kingdom had changed their leaders. That showed how global politics is into a wave of change of leadership.

From the Netherlands to the Philippines, citizens voted down the ruling parties to put a new government with the hope of change and good governance.

In Indonesia, it was not so. Garnering over 60% of the votes in a three-cornered fight, Susilo Bambang Yudhoyono (SBY) convincingly won the presidential election in the first round. Aside from shunning a possible second round, SBY also defied the international wave of opposition win in national elections characterized as free and fair.

Most incumbents were able to hold on to power in national elections marred with fraud and irregularities. But SBY did it in a free and fair election of the third biggest democracy voting only the second time in a direct election of its leader. He won his first term in the second round in 2004 election.

Outside Indonesia, there has been a surge of opposition winning national elections. In neighboring Australia and New Zealand, both rejected the incumbents in their run for reelection. In November 2007, Australians voted for Kevin Rudd of Labor over the reelectionist John Howard of Liberal. Then a year after that, New Zealand chose John Key of National Party over the incumbent Helen Clark of Labor Party.

In East Asia, South Korea put the conservative Lee Myung-bak to power, dispensing the ruling liberals at the helm. Then in 2008, the popular election of Barack Obama of the Democrats for the US presidency over the ruling Republican candidate highlighted the ascent of opposition to power. Then in march 2009, the opposition win in El Salvador capped the first time the left-leaning party Farabundo Marti National Liberation Front (FMNLF) came to power.

The incumbents who won elections in their country were faced by accusations of electoral fraud. In Iran and

Afghanistan, the sitting presidents were declared winners of the elections, but with doubt and protests among their citizens. Iran particularly faced the largest series of protests only seen during the 1979 revolution.

However, SBY calmly and handily shook up the allegations of fraud. The magnitude of his win silenced the opposition's claims of irregularities. His composure as a military man was resounding in the ways he handled terrorism threats in his country. It would be noted that Indonesia was the site of brazen and bold terrorist's attacks by bombings in the capital Jakarta and Bali where hundreds of foreigners died.

The global financial crisis somehow has not deterred the Indonesian economy from performing well. It is the only Southeast Asian country to be part of the G20, a group of developed and emerging economies in the world.

Now, SBY is etched in the history of his country as the man of the hour. He has to perform as Indonesians expect him to usher the country into a better environment and future.

This is the time to calm down the fears and worries of the public on the economy and politics. Most incumbents have failed them. They are looking at the opposition for alternatives. Otherwise, the public will find solace in their own power to direct their lives.

Violent student protests: A sign of the times?

Today is neither the best nor the worst of times. But the signs of the times are leaning towards the latter.

We oftentimes see workers, women, farmers, fisher folk, drivers, professionals, urban poor, youth and students demonstrating on the streets and picket lines. Protests are peoples' expressions of their freedom, idealism, struggles and frustrations in life.

Because they are free, they choose to take their grievances to the streets. Because they are driven by an image of what should be, they propose alternatives to the current situation. Because they are struggling, they are pressed to demand their rights. Because they are frustrated, they start to question and challenge the system and regime.

Protests are one measure of a functioning democracy. In autocratic regimes protests are banned and outlawed. Since democracy is the rule of the majority represented by elected officials, influencing the majority through protests is a legal, accepted and sensible thing to do. Protests also signify the desire of people to take part in governance. They represent people's claims to their representative government.

Much has been said about student protests lately. Condemning students' protests as such is to denounce a significant part of our history. What we are now, what we enjoy now, can be attributed to student protests during past repressive regimes, including the colonial years.

Student protest is powered by young people. Studies show that the psychology of young people tends to disregard existing public norms and order. Last month's images of tearing down a wall, smashing car windows and turning over and burning a car are images of a lack of rules and disorder. Other studies show young people can view public norms on law and order as restricting and constraining.

Last week, students saw a metal fence as something that restricted them from the halls of decision-making, the House of Representatives and the State Palace. They saw it as something that had to be torn down to enable them to participate or to have a say in decision-making. The smashing of windows was the demand for transparency.

It was the urge to see what was inside. The turning over and burning of the car symbolized the students' contempt of the current situation. It was also a show of strength and power to demonstrate with their own hands their blazing frustration.

The violence in this specific student protest highlighted the level of their frustration with the existing state of society, law and order. Students usually regard government as representing the context, law and order within which they take action.

In peace and conflict studies, there is a theory known as relative deprivation. It explains violence occurs when a group feels deprived of something another group has. In this case, students almost always feel that they are deprived of their ideals and rights as citizens by their government. The students and elected and appointed officials in the government are all citizens of this country.

However, the House and the Palace have the power to decide on national issues that affect everyone. This power is deprived from the students. They feel the real power and right to decide should be rightfully in the people's hands, their hands. Last week, they simply exercised that power and right.

The violence in student protests can also be a sign of the times, moving to worse times in terms of economics. This will become a political issue if the government fails to act on the expressed need and will of its deprived people.

I dread the day when students will be joined by workers, drivers, women, farmers, fisher folk, professionals, urban poor and the middle class on the streets. It will be massive. And it could change government direction and the future and rewrite the history of the country, just like in 1998.

Or am I reading the signs too far ahead and from too far away? Then, who else will?

Contemporary violence and our government is at it

Without understanding the very thing we want to prevent and stop -- violence -- peace will remain elusive.

Aimed to address global violence, the Second World Peace Forum, sponsored by Muhammadiyah, the Cheng Ho Foundation and the Center for Dialogue and Cooperation among Civilizations (CDCC) and held in Jakarta on June 24-26, concluded with a number of calls and appeals.

One of which is to return to the basic teachings of one's religion. It is premised in the belief that each religion promotes and spreads peace. Another call is for all religions to play an active role in combating both direct and structural violence through their own communities and groups.

Based on news reports, various speakers at the forum presented a host of forces that cause violence in the world today. One speaker attributed the continuing and growing violence to superpowers like the United States, Russia and Germany, which produce large numbers of arms and weapons. These arms and weapons usually supply the arms and weaponry needs of groups in conflict.

Most speakers followed familiar scripts, saying that religion has a role in preventing and stopping violence. Others said that violence is not a "religious problem". Rather, it has to be looked at as a human rights issue. One related interview pointed out that the politicization of religion causes violence. When religion is used for non-religious purposes, that is when violence occurs.

In the end, there was a unified call and appeal urging religious leaders to highlight common issues that incite violence such as poverty, injustice, human rights abuse and discontent, among others, instead of stressing the differences of belief that divide communities.

Interestingly in the same city where the peace forum was being held, there were violent protests led by students on the streets. Thousands of students were demanding to scrap the order to increase fuel prices and the release of their detained comrades. They were able to pull down part of the fence around the House of Representatives' compound. The tearing down of the fence was a symbolic fall of public order that day. Dozens of protesters were arrested and some properties were vandalized and destroyed. One police car was burned by protesters.

The violent scenes in Jakarta are a replay of what's happening on streets around the world. Lately, the world has seen protests turn violent in South Korea, Thailand, India, Pakistan, Nepal, China and even in European countries. Clashes between protesters and police have resulted to injuries on both sides. Sometimes, opposing protesters collided.

I think protests and responses to protests by authorities and their supporters are forms of contemporary violence.

Does religion play a role in this contemporary violence? Thus far, it does not and hopefully will not.

South Koreans took to the streets to resist a beef-import deal between their government and the United States. The Thais went to the streets to show their opposition to the newly elected government acting as a proxy for ousted former prime minister Thaksin. Indians mobbed the streets to protest soaring fuel prices.

This was the same reason for Indonesians, Nepalese, Spaniards, French and other Europeans to hold picket lines and smash windows of the trucks or cars of those drivers uncooperative with their aim.

Pakistanis toured the streets and burned effigies of President Musharraf to force him to resign and to call for the reinstatement of expelled judges. Tibetans in Nepal gathered to demonstrate their resistance to the rule of China in their homeland. Chinese protesters torched a government building and cars to denounce a ruling by officials about the mysterious death of a student.

What we are witnessing is violence on the streets brought about by political and/or economic dynamics, and not by religion. Protesters nowadays are political and/or economic beings. They are not religious ones.

Protesters demand participatory governance and transparency in South Korea, accountability in Thailand, subsidies and tax breaks on fuel prices in India, Indonesia,

Nepal and European countries, accountability and judicial independence in Pakistan, autonomy and/or independence in Nepal by Tibetans, and liability and the end of corruption in China.

Since the contemporary violence that we have now is political and economic in nature and consequence, it can apparently be addressed by the government. Unfortunately, the government is a party to the contemporary violence.

Students outside the Gedung Kesenian Jakarta performing their own arts in protest of the formal and exclusive event of ASEAN Performing Arts in 2008

Stampede for the excesses of the wealthy: social injustice in our midst

The exasperating scenes of elderly women gasping for air and space have been beamed into our collective memories and consciousness through the power of the media (e.g. TV and newspapers).

This tragedy has touched a strand of humanity in and among us. The death of 21 poor women in a stampede to get Rp 30,000 worth of alms from a rich family in Pasuruan, East Java, is very saddening.

Who would not be moved by images of elderly women succumbing to these external forces that pushed them to that excruciating end?

They were helplessly struggling, grasping and longing for something that was not theirs. And then, some of them gave up struggling. They stopped grasping and longing for something that was not theirs.

In the end, 21 women lost their lives. For all we know, these women might have been struggling, grasping and longing their whole lives.

What is the value of Rp 20,000 or Rp 30,000?

The elderly women have their own calculations, beyond our standards and economic understanding. They know its worth more than the giver, economist or anyone who has millions or billions of rupiah.

There is no doubt in my mind that what happened last Sept. 15 was violence. It was both direct and structural violence. Direct violence occurs when physical harm is done. Structural violence, on the other hand, happens when harmful conditions are created for some sectors of population which are marginalized and disadvantaged.

Notably, victims of these kinds of violence are normally the elderly, women, children and minorities. Our society today is characterized by unjust and unequal structures that engender and cause violence. When politicians steal money from the coffers of the government, they deprive the elderly, women, children and minorities from adequate and responsive social services.

When employers do not give their workers living wages, they deny the rights of workers to a decent living. When governments favor one ethnicity, religion, class or gender, they deny people of those groupings a fighting chance to be productive and contribute to national development or to work with and for their own governments.

These narratives present systemic violence of societal unjust and unequal structures. Their justification and rationalization may be difficult to ponder, but the existence of these structures could not be denied. One does not have to be a genius to point out the obvious results of these unjust and unequal structures. This is why, evidently, the world is mired and engulfed with exploitation, human rights violations, violence, landlessness and a lack of access to social services.

Even our relationships with others are shaped by these structures. Some examples of these relationships are the unfair labor practices of an employer toward his or her workers; substandard services to our clients or customers; manipulative and abusive treatment of our partners, friends or family members; and a superior view of ourselves compared to others.

What makes a violent structure are these hierarchical relationships and vertical inequalities that tip the balance of power and impede the satisfaction of basic human needs of others.

The gap between the rich and poor is widening. It is not that the poor are not trying real hard to eke out a decent living and extricate themselves from abject poverty. It is that certain societal structures limit their options and opportunities for social mobilization and gainful activities.

While the hierarchical relationships between and among social groups are enduring and strongly embedded in a social system, structural change needs to create social strain, conflict and disequilibrium between and among groups to make the relationships more horizontal.

The Sept. 15 tragedy may be the necessary strain and trigger point to inspire and motivate people to struggle against structural violence. A structural change will entail an action and task that necessitates purposive and cognitive behavior.

The first task is networking -- which links to outside the oppressive structure. Civil society groups can potentially be links for the poor.

Second is political education which can adopt Freire's *conscientization* (critical consciousness). Education of this kind will bring empowerment in their midst. Third is mobilization which is characterized by a collective action to challenge the unjust and unequal relationships and social arrangement.

We are moved by the death of the 21 poor women, to reconfigure and rethink our own relationships with others -- especially those in need; and to challenge the structures that make our elderly women queue for long hours and sacrifice their lives.

We cannot and should not be part of these structures that bring violence to our women and children. We should be building structures that are just and fair, and that make it unnecessary to queue and beg for something that we are already entitled to.

Celebrating the day as a new nation to a birth of a new region

In August 2008, I was in Jakarta, Indonesia celebrating the Independence Day (Hari Kemerdekaan) with the villagers in Mampang Prapatan, Jakarta Selatan. It was a fun-filled and grassroot celebration of games and dancing to mark an important day in the history of the nation.

Sixty-five years ago, Indonesia gained its independence from the Dutch authority. It was to mark the birth of a new nation, rebuilding it with its own peoples' creative minds and determined hands, according to its own design, identity, and aspiration. Nationalism was at its peak. The pride of being Indonesian and of all that was Indonesian reverberated in the bones and marrows of those who waited, struggled, and won for the newly-independent nation. That was sixty-three years ago.

After sixty-three years, is Indonesia getting closer to the design that the proponents of independent Indonesia have imagined? Does the nation's current situation have a tinge of their aspiration? Have the peoples become more Indonesian or less? These questions are necessary to rethink and reflect on the direction of the country. But it is likewise necessary to consider who we are, historically and culturally, if we want to discern what our place in this globalizing world is.

Indonesia is composed of multiethnic and multireligious population. The mosaic of the country is rooted in the variety of food and languages, diversity of performing arts and customs, wealth of heritage and history, and archipelagic landscape. There is so much to be proud of in the country. And that pride is entrenched in the hearts and minds of Indonesians and expressed in their daily lives.

Remember sixty-three years ago. Indonesia should never be the same as it was.

This year saw the declaration of Kosovo as an independent country. Kosovars who are mainly ethnic Albanians and Muslims celebrated frantically the historic moment of separation from Serbia, a predominantly Christian country. The new republic of Kosovo promised to embrace

32

everyone in Kosovo regardless of their ethnicity and religion. Nationalism drove the peoples of both Kosovo and Serbia on the streets; one celebrating, the other protesting.

Imagine Kosovo sixty-three years from now.

Certainly, Kosovo will be part of the European Union. And most likely, Serbia will also join the EU. Nationalism which drove these two countries to go at each other will be replaced by regionalism which is a key in dealing with the challenges of the globalizing world.

Indonesia is a founding member of ASEAN which has a binding Charter for all member-states to ratify to be integrated more into one dynamic community. Sadly, Indonesia has yet to ratify the ASEAN Charter, along with the Philippines and Thailand. The ASEAN Charter is gearing up the Southeast Asian regional organization towards a rule-based association.

Timor Leste which gained independence from Indonesia in 1999 has expressed its desire to join ASEAN. Both countries have a hostile past of each other. Both will be integrated into one regional organization, one vision, one identity, and one community working for peace, stability and prosperity for the peoples of ASEAN which recently celebrated its 41st founding anniversary.

In the celebration of ASEAN's anniversary, the current Secretary-General of ASEAN, Dr. Surin Pitsuwan, mentioned that the world is excited about the prospects of ASEAN with the Charter at hand. The prospects present a region that can stand and take care of its own affairs effectively and peacefully. That means, "one region less a problem to the world," he said.

As the host country of ASEAN Secretariat and a third of the region's population, Indonesia is vital to the process of attaining the vibrant prospect of ASEAN. Thus, Indonesia's independence must move its design, identity and aspiration towards working with its neighbors, its partners for peace, stability and prosperity in the region. It has to take the lead in the integration bid when other ASEAN members are facing their own internal and political problems.

Like nation-building, regional structures have to start building in the grassroots where people identify themselves. ASEAN can look at the way Indonesians celebrate their

Independence Day. And be inspired from the historical and cultural bond that peoples take pride on.

Statue of Pattimura, a National Hero of Indonesia

Being Indonesian: More or less

When was the last time you felt more Indonesian than ever? As a non-Indonesian, I ask this question because I saw how Kosovo celebrated when its parliament declared their independence from Serbia earlier this year. I also read the news about the celebrations in Mongolia on their winning their first ever Olympic gold medal in Beijing. So, when was it that you felt more Indonesian than ever?

Independence Day on Aug. 17 would have to be one of those moments when you felt good to be Indonesian. Seeing red and white all over the place with Indonesian flags flying high in every corner, on streets, buildings and outside houses. This gives us a sense of identity and belonging. There was hardly any other moment in history which is comparable to Indonesia's declaration of independence.

Winning an Olympic gold would undoubtedly make every Indonesian proud of their own athletes' achievements. And this is exactly what shuttlers Kido and Setiawan did for 225 million Indonesians. They delivered a golden performance for Indonesia in the men's doubles badminton at the Beijing 2008 Olympic Games.

The feat came at the expense of the Chinese team who were playing on their home turf. Any athlete would understand the odds of playing against a home court advantage, but Kido and Setiawan rose to the challenge, winning from behind a set to take the two succeeding sets against a hostile crowd.

Both events combined to make us proud to be Indonesian and gave us a sense of nationalism.

Becoming Indonesian is easy: You could be born of Indonesian parents or be naturalized through a legal process. However, being Indonesian is about much more than this -- much more than simply a nationality or citizenship which can be acquired by fulfilling bureaucratic requirements.

Being Indonesian resides in the core of we are, internalized in history, songs, traditions, institutions, or in the all-encompassing culture. In Freudian terms, being Indonesian is imprinted in the unconscious mind which is reflected in our conscious level.

35

Thus, these two significant events activated internalized meanings and symbolisms attached to being Indonesian -- and this may have been triggered by any number of different scenarios; putting up a flag, singing the national anthem, seeing pictures of heroes or presidents, taking part in local activities, posting a note in friendster or facebook or simply talking with friends and family, here or abroad.

In a critical world, the nation should be grateful for these two historic events. They have reaffirmed and secured the 63-year-old aspirations and goals of the proponents of an independent Indonesia among the young Indonesians who will now see our country through the next 63 years.

However, when a decree was issued banning Ahmadiyah (a religious sect) to observe its beliefs, was the government being more Indonesian? When professionals decide to work abroad and send their remittance back home, are they being less Indonesian than those who decide to practice their professions locally?

When students and businesspeople use English to communicate their ideas and feelings, are they being less Indonesian? When people chose to spend their Independence Day at Ancol with their families, are they less Indonesian than those who went to Monas or took part in other independence related activities?

These sample questions can take us back to the core of what it means to be Indonesian. And it is through continuous questioning and reflection that we will establish what is truly great about being an Indonesian.

Indonesia has celebrated its Independence Day 63 times already.

So what is new? Not much, except that these two events can serve to hold Indonesia and its peoples together and make sense of their special place in the world. Events such as these provide Indonesians with more reasons to celebrate triumphantly.

Our Church, our refuge

We oftentimes see a church as a landmark. More than that, it is a refuge to many who are weary and longing for home and direction in life.

Coming from a predominantly Catholic country, I grew up in a community where it took me just seven minutes to walk to the nearest church. I studied in Naga City, Philippines where churches are part of its landscape and tourist attractions. Hence, I always suppose that a church is always within reach, anytime, anywhere in the world.

Staying in a new place is mystifying at times. The foreign and strange surroundings can unmask the deep and unsettling sense of longing for the familiar and comfortable world. This is my story when I stayed in Costa Rica and Jakarta, Indonesia.

When I went to Costa Rica for my graduate studies, the nearest *iglesia* or church was only 15 minutes away. That church is located in downtown Ciudad Colon. Literally, I had to walk down from my house going to the church, since my place is situated on a higher part of the town.

Like the Philippines, Costa Rica is predominantly Catholic. I even went "church-hopping" one weekend in the neighboring cantons of Piedades and Sta. Ana, and the city of San Jose. I noticed that churches in Costa Rica put a barrier after a few steps from the main entrance facing the altar. I think the purpose is to avoid disturbances and distractions from outside. Thus, from outside, no one could see the altar and pulpit. This setup discourages parishioners to stay outside while attending masses. This also somehow evokes a sense of sacredness and heavenly feeling once inside, shut from the worldly temptations outside, but welcoming the worried and restless hearts and souls inside the church.

In the Philippines, some people stay outside the church while attending Sunday Mass. This is evident in almost every church where people are spilling over the confines of the building. Crowded during Sunday masses, our century-old churches could not accommodate the growing number of parishioners. This gives reason and justification for people to stay outside while attending mass. Besides, there is no barrier a few steps from the main entrance, and there are both attractions and distractions outside.

I think that for Catholics, experiencing a new place meaningfully would not be complete without dropping by at a nearby church for a blessing, prayer or mass.

For more than three months, I stayed in a predominantly Muslim country — Indonesia. Ubiquitously, mosques are common sights in the country. As a matter of fact, behind my house, there is a mosque. Halfway from my house to the bus way, there is another one. Outside a mall, beside a hotel, across a cathedral, Muslims have plenty of choices to go to and have no reasons to miss prayer time.

As a stranger in a foreign country, I did not know exactly where to go to attend Sunday mass. That caused me to shell out Rp 17,000 (P80) or less than $2 to buy a map of Jakarta City. With a map, I searched for gerejas (churches) near my place in Mampang Prapatan, Jakarta Selatan. There was none in a circumference of two kilometers. But I saw a number of crosses in the map that indicated and marked Catholic churches. That saved me from looking further.

When I saw in the map that there is a cathedral in Jakarta (of course, there is!), I immediately planned my first weekend to visit it.

After few days in Jakarta, the Gereja Ketedral Jakarta was the first church I visited in the megacity. A one-hour bus ride and a ten minute-walk from the nearest bus station were worth all the planning and effort to actually see it. The cathedral looks magnificently imposing. Its gothic-style is a beauty to behold. Something pricked my chest when I stepped inside the church compound after having difficulty crossing the street from the opposite side. I stayed outside the majestic structure for a while, marveling its presence within my reach.

It was Saturday afternoon. There was a photo shoot in front of the church by a couple wearing wedding dresses. They looked so happy together, so natural together, in person and, I guess, in pictures too. Obviously, they felt blessed to be together.

The couple reminded me of….. ahhh.. love… it makes me wonder what I have been missing all this time.

Then, as if welcoming me, the door opened. Entering, I passed by the couple and smiled at them, appreciating their presence. At last, I was inside a church in Indonesia. My restlessness calmed down. A certain ethereal feeling enveloped me. I needed to sit. But I knelt. I was overwhelmed by the weight of my body. I had travelled for more than an hour just to reach this hallowed place. Silently, I prayed, thankful of the moment, of the whole walk, of many things, pouring my heart out to the One I long for.

Walking outside, I did not look back. Smiling wryly, I brought the cathedral with me. And my heart and soul found sanctuary in the bustling city of Jakarta, Indonesia.

Jakarta Cathedral, standing right in front of the Istiqlal Mosque

Motorcycles easy on Jakarta Streets

Let me begin by saying that I have been a pedestrian for so long as I could remember, and I am proud of it. Pedestrians, unite and walk!

One thing I could not miss noticing in Jakarta is the ubiquitous motorcycles. Every morning when I am on the way to ASEAN by a Metro Mini (mini-bus Jakarta style), a herd of black helmet and jacket-wearing motorcycle riders swarms the streets of the eight-lane Mampang Prapatan up to the four-lane Kap Tendean. Mampang Prapatan's two-lanes in the middle are reserved for the exclusive use of TransJakarta buses.

One good thing about the Metro Mini buses is that they are loads of them with designated numbers. My bus is number 75. I have not seen number 1 though. But I saw number 610. There must be lots of them here. Creatively, they have the same color (combination of orange and blue). That's why I don't have to miss my number or else I will get somewhere in Jakarta, not my destination. I think I should try to be somewhere I don't know. Hmmmmm...

There is another Metro Mini buses named Kopaja. They are colored green and white. They have numbers too. They distract me whenever I am looking and waiting for my bus 75. I have the bus number on my wallet, cellfone, notebook, and on the first day, on my palm. Great way not to forget huh! Trust me, it works.

Anyway, from my house, I ride on a motorcycle or I have to walk 25 minutes in a "business causal" attire. Wow, you should see how Jakarta has changed me! I look good and feel good. Believe me, otherwise you're not my friend. Coincidentally, "Yakob" usually drives me to the busway. It costs me 5,000 rupiahs (1 peso = 200 rupiahs). It costs me more than riding a Metro Mini which charges 2,500 rupiahs. When "Yakob" learned that I am Filipino, he immediately blurted with a closed fist while driving, "Manny Pacquiao." He loves Pacquiao more than I do, I think. What's not to love in Pacquiao? He won again another title. This time in the lightweight division, and distinguishing himself as the only

Asian to win championship titles in four different weight divisions.

Every corner of the streets in Mampang area has a pool of motorcycles waiting for passengers to take them somewhere. In my house, there are seven motorcycles and five cars parked inside the compound. We are, in my unofficial count, 15 tenants in the house. So only me and two more pedestrians who do not drive a fuel-powered transportation machine.

Based on a news report in Kompas June 6, 2008, there were about 45,948,747 motorcycles in Indonesia in 2007. It is almost 46 million motorcycles spread across the archipelago. With 222.1 million population, Indonesia has 1 motorcycle for every 5 persons. So Indonesia is basically running on motorcycles.

Whenever I go, I see very few people walk on the sidewalks or streets of Jakarta. Motorcycles become people's convention to move from one place to another. I understand that motorcycles move fast and can navigate the streets on their own way. Besides, they consume less gas than cars.

In the portion of Jakarta where I pass, deserted sidewalks are typical scenes. I and Biney (my classmate and co-intern in ASEAN) use the sidewalk with ease and leisure in the afternoon for strolling, under the shade of trees and cloud of gas-smoke. I look around.

Where have all the pedestrians gone?